# Cheetah

# Cheetah

Kathrine and Karl Ammann

Foreword by Stefanie Powers

ARCO PUBLISHING, INC.
New York

## Acknowledgments

Many people have helped us in our cheetah study and in preparing this book. Those deserving special mention are Mohamed Amin, Ishitiaq Chaudry, Cornelius and Barbara Dutcher, Alex Furrer, Don Hunt, John Naiguren and Daniel Sindiyo. To all we express our gratitude and sincere thanks.

Edited by Ian Parker

Design by Craig Dodd

Published by Arco Publishing, Inc.
215 Park Avenue South, New York, NY 10003

© Camerapix, K & K Ammann 1985

Library of Congress Catalog  Card Number:

84–70999

ISBN 0–668–06259–2

Printed in Hong Kong

# Contents

# Foreword

Cheetahs are by far and away the swiftest things on four legs. But this delightful book shows that they have many other charms. Cheetahs are not only swift and deadly killers but lovable creatures, with a gentleness that other species of big cats do not possess.

It is not uncommon to find them kept as household pets in some of the old bush farmhouses of Kenya. Guests at one of the houses outside Nairobi would often sit down on a cheetah skin sofa – only to discover that it was alive! The owner kept three or four of these giant tabbies around the house, and their purrs of contentment sounded like the hum of a small workshop. Most of us will never have that disconcerting – but pleasant and memorable – experience. But we can all get to know and admire, if not love, this feline of the African savanna through the pages of this remarkable book.

The survival of this species, and all endangered species, is the goal of the William Holden Wildlife Foundation. The Foundation was established to further the work and dreams of a man whose love for African wildlife and devotion to its preservation instilled that same love in the people he touched. I was one of the lucky few.

Since Bill was a founder of the Mount Kenya Game Ranch now operated by co-founder Don Hunt, it is fitting that the William Holden Wildlife Education Center should be located here. Don and his wife Iris have spent years in captive wildlife breeding programs, and have raised many orphaned cheetahs. Their experience is invaluable to the work of the Foundation.

I have worked with Don, Iris and Bill for the cause of conservation of Kenya's – and all of Africa's – wildlife, of which the cheetah is an integral and most fascinating part. I am delighted to contribute the Foreword to this commendable book, which brings the story of the cheetah to life with a grace and poetry as extraordinary as the animal itself. I hope you will enjoy this book as much as I have, and as much as, clearly, Karl and Kathrine have enjoyed researching, photographing and writing it.

*Stefanie Powers*

Stefanie Powers, Chairman
William Holden Wildlife Foundation

Mount Kenya Game Ranch
Nanyuki, Kenya

June 4, 1984

In fear, a cheetah cub stares from the midst of a thicket in
which he sought shelter after being chased by a lion.

# Introduction

To us, cheetahs are the most beautiful of cats. Their long legs, slender bodies, small rounded heads, striking coats and fluid movements elevate them to an elegance above all other carnivores. Their amber eyes sweep through the human observer with an imperial, feline hauteur, yet despite their aloofness the species seems to lack the elemental savagery that is so prominent a feature of the other great cats. Efficient hunters that they are, cheetahs nonetheless appear to be more gentle, 'civilized' predators than lions, leopards and tigers. It has been our good fortune to have studied cheetahs in the wild for nearly two years. During that time we tried to record our observations photographically. The results form the basis of this book. We hope that, in a small way, it will widen knowledge about cheetahs and stimulate interest in their conservation.

In this scientific age, most biological studies are undertaken by those with specific training in zoology. We were thus lucky, as laymen, to have had the opportunity and privilege of being able to watch cheetahs and live close by them in one of Africa's most spectacular wildlife sanctuaries – the Masai Mara Game Reserve in Kenya. The seeds of our interlude there were sown before our marriage in 1980. Karl had worked in Kenya between 1974 and 1976. In his spare time and over holidays he visited the country's game reserves and national parks. These trips gave rise to two conflicting trends; on the one hand he felt a growing fascination with wildlife, on the other a rising sense of frustration. Kenya's parks and game reserves accommodate large numbers of tourists, who are ferried about, bus-load after chattering bus-load, in an atmosphere of pure commercialism. Each bus driver or tour leader is ever on the look-out for stationary vehicles on the premise that they will have stopped to look at something worth watching. Understandable and economical as this method of finding animals no doubt is, game viewing degenerates into driving from one mini-bus agglomeration to the next! When Karl attempted to be independent it was of little use, for as soon as he had stopped to watch an animal, it was only a matter of minutes before others had gathered round to share in what he had found. In such circumstances the sense of being in the wild was as ersatz as the safari parks of the industrial nations in Europe and North America. Karl became haunted by a quote from the eminent zoologist, George Schaller, in his book *Serengeti, A Kingdom of Predators*:

'I cherished my escape from the organised lunacy of life in the city to the elemental complexity of the wilderness. Yesterday, today, and tomorrow became as one as I lived for the moment only, seeking a sense of unity with the earth, the animals. As weeks and months passed, I learned to recognise many of the lions and other predators. Ceasing to be mere animals, they became individuals about whose problems I worried and whose future I anticipated. They became part of my memories of an austere and seemingly harsh land in which man seems of no consequence until he imperceptibly becomes a part of it. This life of isolation, of spending hours alone each day with animals, was part reality, part illusion, and it suited me; it was neither a denial of life nor a retreat from those I loved, but a way of sustaining a sense of spiritual independence. Solitude provokes reflection, and the study became a quest for understanding, not just of the predators but also of myself, a personal *corrida*.'

How could he, too, experience what Schaller wrote of? How could he come to terms with the wild? Clearly short visits to the game parks, basing oneself in the tourist lodges and adopting the commercial routines, could only give the most superficial glimpses of Schaller's Africa. The only way to know wilderness is to actually live within it. And thus was born a dream to do this one day. When we married the dream was shared between us.

Too many of today's personal ambitions are relegated to the never-never land of retirement. The great goals of one's youth, the visits to be made, the experiences to be savoured, are kept as hopes to be fulfilled in the twilight years at the close of a working career. By then, enthusiasms have lost their temper and energies have flagged to the point when the ambitions from youth lose their lustre. We decided to sacrifice immediate career prospects in favour of getting into Africa's wildernesses while our dream was still bright. Our goal was to be allowed to live in or near one of the great game areas and this meant either in or close to one of the national parks or reserves. We knew that this would not be easy. However we were prepared to work for the privilege and were financially independent. Fortune smiled on us for our enquiries coincided with a proposal to translocate some sixty captive cheetah from Namibia to boost Kenya's population of the species. But the Kenya Department of Wildlife Conservation and Management was not convinced that this would serve a useful purpose and, in any case, needed further information on local numbers and their space requirements before accepting the offer. It was agreed that we could help by collecting information on local cheetahs. Our good luck was further enhanced when we were told that we should do so in the Masai Mara Game Reserve, one of the most fertile and scenically attractive in all Africa.

After our initial reconnaissance to Kenya we returned to Europe to equip ourselves for the Mara. We had decided to drive out via Egypt and the Sudan. For the trip we acquired two four-wheel drive vehicles, spares, service and repair manuals, camping equipment and such books on predators in general and cheetahs in particular as we could lay hands on. We arranged for two friends, Helmut Scholtz and Ingrid Ganssman, to accompany us and to drive our second car on the journey to Kenya. On November 2nd 1980 both vehicles with two tonnes of baggage were loaded on the ferry at Ancona, Italy. Four days later they were unloaded in Alexandria onto African soil for the first time.

The overland journey from Alexandria to Nairobi warrants a book to itself. Our route took in Suez, the Red Sea coast, Luxor, the Aswan dam, the Nile Valley, and across the Nubian desert on compass headings to Khartoum. The heat, dust, and, rough tracks (or their complete absence) were uncomfortable and tough on the vehicles. However, these hardships were more than compensated for by the Nile Valley and desert scenery, and the unbelievable hospitality of people in the northern Sudan. In Khartoum there was virtually no fuel for our vehicles. Despite plying the black market for ten days we could only accumulate half the quantity that we estimated necessary to get us to the Kenya border. Nevertheless we set off southwards, hoping that we could beg, borrow or buy the balance that we needed *en route*.

From Khartoum a tarred road ran alongside the Nile to the river port of Kosti. The journey was exhilarating after the trackless desert. Our euphoria evaporated, however, on learning that the road south from Kosti was still closed by the Nile's annual flooding. We could proceed on a much longer route via Wau in the west, but were advised that the fuel shortage there was far worse than in Khartoum. The remaining alternative was to put the vehicles on the river steamer and go south up the Nile to Juba. This we decided to do to conserve our precious fuel.

The steamer trip was right out of the early decades of this century. The vessel was old, very old. Its antiquated appearance was enhanced, not only by its threshing stern paddlewheel, but also by the flotilla of five large barges that it pushed or dragged along with it. For all the world the steamer and its barges looked like a small, bizarre, floating village, for they carried some six hundred men, women and children on their way to the southern Sudan. Some were Southerners going home from employment in the north, others Northerners going south on various errands and yet others a miscellany of travellers going about their ways. Most families' belongings included beds, kitchen equipment and occasionally domestic animals as well. This colourful, noisy, improbable community being dragged up the silent, slumbrous Nile through the interminable sudd and wild scenery, seemed far removed from the twentieth century. *This* was the Africa of the past, of legend and dusty libraries. *These* were the scenes of romance that spawned the tales of Rider Haggard and Tarzan and created the images of Africa that lodged in Hollywood and, ultimately, in our childhood minds. However, this book is about cheetahs and reminiscences about the Nile and its fascinations must await another time and place.

After two weeks afloat we arrived in Juba with adequate fuel to drive on into Kenya, which we did without delay. On this last leg of the journey we experienced the other side of the Sudanese coin. For all its colourful people and attractions, the southern Sudan is still a land of many diseases. Though modern drugs may have established a defence of sorts against the plagues and poxes that challenge newcomers so virulently, the barrier is thin and still frequently breached. When we arrived in Nairobi eight weeks after setting wheels on African soil four thousand five hundred kilometres (2,800 miles) to the north, all four of us were in the grips of malaria.

With proper medical attention we soon recovered our health, however. Bidding Ingrid and Helmut farewell, we set off westwards to the Mara Game Reserve some two hundred kilometres away. We arrived there on December 21st 1980 to commence a two-year study of *Acinonyx jubatus*, alias the spotted one, alias the cheetah, that most elegant of cats.

Right: The Nile, blessed relief in a harsh environment. Despite the possibility of crocodiles and bilharzia (a water-borne disease common in the Nile) and the stares of startled local people, we plunged into its waters in ecstasy after the desert crossing.

Overleaf: The Nile steamer that plies between Kosti and Juba. Virtually a floating village, this leisurely but far from comfortable form of transport recalls the romance of bygone eras.

Following pages: Elephant in Mara's golden grasslands.

*1 · The Mara*

The Mara Game Reserve comprises just under 1,400 km² (about 545 square miles) and is roughly rectangular in shape, with the Kenya–Tanzania international border forming its southern boundary. Immediately across the border lies the great Serengeti National Park. To the wild animals of the region, oblivious to human politics and designs, the Mara and Serengeti are one and they freely move between them. Ecologically, the Mara Reserve is the northernmost extension of the Serengeti. In political terms the Reserve belongs to the Masai people, and it is administered on their behalf by Kenya's Department of Wildlife Conservation and Management. These pastoral people surround the Reserve to west, north and east and, again, the animals do not distinguish between where humans may or may not graze their stock. Thus they cross the Reserve boundaries at will and go among the Masai herds as they have for centuries.

The Reserve takes its name from the Mara river which flows from north to south through the Reserve's western half. In turn the river may take its name from the nature of the country through which it flows, for the term 'mara' in the Masai tongue means patchy and could refer to the extensive clumps of bush, forest and thicket that, forty years ago and more, were characteristic of what is now the Reserve. Be that as it may, the majority of these patches of dense vegetation have been destroyed by elephants and fire. Today only vestiges of this vegetation remain. For the greater part, the Mara Reserve is open grassland with areas of scattered bush and light woods. The country undulates gently and water courses and occasional streams all flow towards the Mara river. It is along the river and the permanent streams that the remnants of forest occur. The general openness of the area makes it easy to drive about and an ideal place in which to watch wildlife. The altitude of the Reserve is around 5,000 feet above sea level so although it is almost on the equator, its climate is temperate and equable. Heavy rains fall in April and December, but some rain falls in almost every month of the year so that the harshness of the 'dry' seasons is less pronounced than in most other areas of East Africa.

The vast numbers of grazing animals that use the Mara grasslands are perhaps its most striking feature. Today this concentration is probably as great as it ever could have been in times gone by, and is certainly far more spectacular than it was during the first five decades of this century. When it first became known to white men some eighty years ago, the Mara was not open grassland as it is today. Then, elephant were not numerous. By the nineteen-fifties they were clearly increasing and as this trend proceeded these animals broke up woods and thickets, letting in flammable grasses. In the drier times of the year fires, started far beyond the Mara's environs, swept through the grassland and further eroded the elephant-damaged thickets. As the forest and thicket diminished so, too, did the tsetse flies that had lived in them and which, previously, had kept the Masai and their cattle at bay. The closer the Masai came to the Mara, the more frequent the fires became, for they burn to improve pasture for their stock. And so it went, the influence of elephants, men and fires opened up the country across the Mara and deep into the woodlands of the northern Serengeti. As the grassland spread, so the grazing animals have thrived. Those prospering most of all are the wildebeest which have risen in numbers from about three hundred thousand in the early nineteen-sixties to close to two million today. An unforgettable experience in July 1981 was the arrival of the migration. Fully two days before the wildebeest appeared, we could hear them; nasal grunts and bleats from thousands upon thousands of them blended into a dull background sound, vaguely reminiscent of surf on a far-distant shore. It is when the migration is 'in' that the Mara reaches its annual peak as one of the modern world's greatest wildlife spectacles.

The Serengeti-Mara's other grazers have also increased in a similar, if not quite such spectacular, fashion: the gazelles, zebras, buffaloes and many others. Since the Mara is the best watered and most fertile part of the whole ecosystem, the vast concourse of grazers tends to gather there through much of the year's drier months.

With the increase of herbivores it is logical to assume that there has been a parallel rise in the fortunes of those that prey on them: lions, leopards, hyaenas, jackals and of course the subject of our particular interest, cheetahs. Thus the golden openness of the grasslands, the ease of access generally, the abundance of wild animals, large and small, predators and prey, glorious scenery and wonderful climate, all combine to make the Mara a magnificent environment in which to live and study nature.

Our base in the Mara was under a large fig tree on the Talek river, close to where it crossed the Reserve's northern boundary. Life under canvas was novel, but we were introduced to it by an old safari hand, Daudi, who had years of experience on the luxury hunting safaris that were once such a feature of East African tourism. Under his tutelage we quickly learned that life in the bush could be as comfortable as anyone might wish for. The centre-piece of our camp was a large dining or mess tent which served as a general living room. Close by were two 'Manyara' bedroom tents that, with their plastic floors and gauze-screened windows, could be zipped up and rendered virtually insect-proof. There was also a kitchen tent and Daudi's accommodation alongside. Lighting was provided by kerosene lamps. Cold storage depended on a temperamental paraffin refrigerator. Of course there was no running water so our bathroom tent was placed as close to the river's edge as possible in order to minimize the distance water had to be carried. Hot water could be drawn from an old aviation fuel drum under which we lit a wood fire, and one could choose to wash either under a shower hanging from a branch of the fig tree, or in a canvas bath. The pride of our small tented settlement was the toilet, a canvas closet sited on a ridge thirty paces or so behind the living quarters. From this the user could look over a wide vista of the plains and meditate on the wildlife moving about them. The lavatory functioned on the 'safari dry-flush' system. In this a comfortable seat was set over a deep hole and a bucket of wood ash from the campfires substituted for the water of the urban pull and let-go cistern.

Our tents were second-hand, bought from a professional hunter whose clients formed a list of the famous and wealthy straight out of *Who's Who*. No doubt his tales about the tents' travels and former inhabitants were part of a sales pitch to dispose of the equipment after hunting was banned in Kenya; but they contained strong elements of truth. People often puzzle over why the world's wealthy so frequently endured the 'rigours' of safari and surmise that comfort in the bush can only be secured at great expense. In our life under canvas we learned how attractive camping can be, how comfort may be achieved cheaply and why the delights and simplicity of dwelling in the bush proved so appealing to the world's elite.

Socially we were not lonely. Friends came from Nairobi and elsewhere to visit us and share camp life. Others resident in or about the Mara, fellow researchers, tourist lodge staff or government officials, used to drop in for meals. However, if they came for dinner it usually meant that they stayed for the night, too, for no one was supposed to drive about the Reserve after dark.

There were of course some disadvantages to living on the banks of the Talek. We learned early that some wildlife is distinctly hostile. Foremost among such species were driver ants – locally known as 'siafu' or safari ants. If anything epitomized mindless, efficient cruelty – the nether pole of nature – these insects did. Their society is based upon a queen and a community of soldiers and workers that come in a variety of models, the largest of which are nearly two centimetres long. All seem to have a frightful commitment to bite whatever moves. Each community has a territory that may encompass several acres, within which it will have a number of subterranean bases. At any one time, the whole community will be operating from one of these depots, sending out foraging parties to bring back food. Principally *siafu* live on termites, but will tackle anything they come across. Woe betide the unfortunate who cannot escape, be it rat, rabbit or much larger, for with surprising rapidity it will be dismantled, jawful by tiny jawful, and taken back to base. When food becomes scarce around one base, the community moves to the next, taking eggs, immatures and the queen with it, and commences foraging on new ground. Unfortunately *siafu* like moist, shady areas best – such as along a river bank. While they could never be considered a danger to humans (save, perhaps, to a helpless babe in a cot) they have provided many painful and uncomfortable experiences. Too often the observer of things above ground has failed to see the carpet of *siafu* below, and the oversight brought to attention by the thousand bites that suddenly ensued on all points between ankle and navel. Equally nasty is to waken at night to find *siafu* throughout the bed. Daudi showed us a simple expedient to prevent such unpleasant occurrences. He dug a shallow trench around every tent and regularly filled it with wood ash, which safari ants do not like crossing.

For most of the year our fig tree provided deep and most welcome shade. In January 1981 it fruited heavily. Wild figs were sought by a host of birds and animals, particularly baboons, who arrived to feast at dawn. Moving about the branches they dislodged shower after shower of soft figs onto our tents and, not being burdened by humanity's concern for hygiene, the unmentionable by-products of yesterday's feasts as well. The green of our tents soon stained to brown. When we tried to dissuade the baboons from using our fig tree, with the aid of a sling shot, they leapt from its branches in alarm. Alack, some jumped on the tents, tearing the canvas in several places. Our trauma only ceased when the fig stopped fruiting.

There were other unwelcome visitors too. Hyaenas were prone to carry away any utensil with traces of food upon it that might have been left lying about, and to sink their teeth into many a plastic or rubber article, testing its edibility. Once a spitting cobra had to be chased from our mess tent, and on another occasion we encountered a large forest cobra in the bush behind our staff tent. Daudi saw it regularly on subsequent days and was so upset that he wished to move his tent elsewhere. Our Masai neighbours, who lived across the river outside the Reserve, advised that salt poured into the snake's hole would do the trick. We never saw the cobra again, though why salt should be a serpent repellant we do not know.

In our early days in camp all was new and none more so than the night noises which, to our unaccustomed ears, were of an almost Hollywood starkness. There was ever a background of insects calling, high-pitched stridulatings and chirpings. Frogs added to this, particularly in the wetter months. The fig tree attracted fruit bats whose noisy squabbling and monotonous, high bell-like 'clink, clink, clink' is so common a feature of the African night. A myriad insectivorous bats squeaked their way through the night, their noise so high-pitched that many cannot hear it. And less constant, but common, were the calls of nightjars and owls. The sounds soon became as much part of the background as traffic sounds are to the town dwellers – constant but unnoticed. Against this aural backdrop there were the greater noises that never failed to register in the mind, regardless of how settled-in we became. When a long way off, lions sounded like distant drum beats, but when close their roaring was astonishing for its volume. The melodious, drawn-out whoop of spotted hyaenas, which starts on a low note and runs through a rising cadence, was so familiar as to almost be the counterpart of an urban clock's chimes. Occasionally, if a kill had been made nearby, we might hear the excited, insane tittering and giggling that hyaenas are famed for. This laughter, as though from a coven of inebriated witches, defies written description. It has to be heard to be appreciated. Perhaps the most sinister of the night sounds, for all that it lacks great volume, was the rough, sawing, grunting of a leopard. It never failed to disturb the baboons who roosted in the tall trees along the river bank near our camp. They, like their fellow primates, men, do not like the dark, and nothing convinced them of this more than hearing that cat with the baleful eyes, calling, unseen, in the dark below.

Sometimes a night was made memorable when lions strolled through the very midst of our camp. Once elephants did likewise and through our gauze-screened window we watched two sniffing some spare tyres. When at ease, they communicated among themselves with deep grumbles and growls and exhibited prodigious and noisy *flatus*. Curiously, and though conscious of the flimsy canvas that separated us from these large and totally wild animals, we seldom felt other than completely secure in our Mara camp. In virtually every way, living in the wilderness proved as satisfying and deeply enjoyable as we had dreamt that it would be.

Vignettes of Mara: the Talek pride of lions close by a
thicket's shade and zebra's dust rising before towering
clouds that, shortly, will lay it with a torrential downpour.

Overleaf: Giraffe in twilight silhouette.

Our camp by the Talek with the migration in the background. The dining tent is in the centre with sleeping tents on either side. Our nearest neighbours were Masai herders who often, illegally but understandably, brought their stock across the Talek into the Mara Reserve and, occasionally, right into our camp.

33

. . . the most sinister of the night sounds, for all that it lacked great volume, was the rough, sawing, grunting of a leopard . . . the cat with the baleful eyes . . .

Kathrine takes a bath on the banks of the Talek.

Overleaf: *Cheetah and Stag with Two Indians* by George Stubbs. Cheetah – Hindi for the Spotted One – were tamed and used to hunt gazelle and deer. The Moghul Emperor, Akbar the Great, is said to have owned one thousand of them. *Manchester City Art Gallery.*

We concluded from the amount of literature on cheetahs that the animal was relatively well-known, at least in laymen's terms. In such circumstances it was unlikely that our study would produce much new to science. However, photography was one field in which we might make worthwhile additions to public knowledge of the species. As far as we were aware, no one had methodically captured all the visual aspects of cheetah behaviour on film. This became our personal goal, in addition to collecting information required by the Department of Wildlife Conservation and Management. Our first step in the study was to familiarize ourselves with what was known about cheetahs in order to recognize the various behaviours. In this chapter we give a synopsis of what we learned from our own observations and the writings of other research workers.

Cheetah derives from a Hindi word – Chita – meaning 'the spotted one' and it gives an inkling that the species once ranged beyond the confines of Africa. And this is true, for in historic times there were wild cheetahs through much of the Middle East, Iran, Afghanistan, Pakistan and north-western India. The fossil record also indicates that both larger and smaller forms once existed in Eurasia. Cheetahs are a branch of the cat family that has specialized in running to secure prey. Common feline characteristics are still apparent in their general form and in many behavioural aspects. Though cheetahs take prey after a long sprint, they try to stalk, cat-like, to within a relatively close distance of fifty metres or so, before starting the high-speed dash for which they are so famous and which has earned them the reputation of being the fastest terrestrial mammals. However, their specialization as runners has called for some modifications in nature's general cat design. They have longer legs and long, supple backs to allow the flexing and great strides that enable them to cover ground at up to 112 km (70 miles) an hour over short distances (the speed has been measured accurately on a greyhound racing track with a cheetah chasing the artifical hare). Their heads are proportionally lighter than in most cat species, again an adaptation in the interests of balance and speed. And with the lighter heads go relatively smaller teeth. Also in the interests of running, the claws are not fully retractile and appear more dog-like than cat-like.

As might be expected with animals that secure their prey through a three-hundred to six-hundred-metre dash, cheetahs are essentially cats of the open. They cannot operate effectively in areas of dense undergrowth, thicket, forest or very tall grass. The animals would not be able to achieve maximum speed if they had to twist and turn among tree boles or over terrain that is uneven or heavily bushed. Thus they are by choice predators of relatively flat lands, which are lightly bushed or wooded with plenty of open space; and, by and large, these are dry lands. Thus it is that cheetah distribution coincides to a substantial degree with the distribution of the old world's gazelles, which are also residents of dry, open, semi-desert and desert country. Cheetahs' strongholds today are the arid lands of Africa between Cape Verde in the west to Gardafui in the east. Further south in and about the Kalahari and in Namibia, where springbok replace the gazelles, cheetahs are again common. In between these northern and southern strongholds, they occur sparingly through the drier and more open of the deciduous woodlands that form so proportion of the vegetation on either side of the Equator. Here and there, as in the islands of cheetahs occur in kinder, more equable climates. In the woodlands where are absent, impala seem to be favoured as prey.

why wild cheetahs became extinct outside Africa and Iran has not been ished. Though they have striking skins, these have never had the softness and touch leopards so attractive a quarry for human hunters. Thus, while coats have been of cheetah skins, the species has never been assiduously hunted for pelts. Cheetahs nid animals that steer clear of people. To our knowledge no case of a man-eater has ever been recorded. Wild cheetahs will bite and scratch if hands are laid upon them, but they are more given to spitting and snarling than to violent action – in marked contrast to their kin, lions, leopards and tigers. We know of no instance in which cheetahs have attacked cattle although they will kill sheep and goats readily if the opportunity arises. However, where flocks are closely tended by shepherds, such predacity is rare. As the pastoralists of African and the Middle Eastern dry lands tend to herd their flocks closely, few seriously consider cheetahs to be vermin. The species probably disappeared outside Africa through the gradual replacement of their wild prey by man's domestic animals and a consequent loss of their food supply.

Tame cheetahs were widely used for hunting in the Middle East, India and even, in medieval times, in some Mediterranean lands. All had to be caught in the wild, for the ancients could not get them to breed in captivity. They were used to course gazelles and the Indian black buck. The sixteenth-century Moghul Emperor, Akbar the Great, is said to have had one thousand cheetahs in his stables. There must have been a large demand for cheetahs and this may have contributed to their decline outside Africa.

Cheetahs' timidity is not only apparent with regard to humans, but also when they are confronted with other predators and scavengers. There are many records of them being driven off their kills by lions, leopards, hyaenas and even jackals and vultures. Indeed this is so pronounced a feature of cheetah behaviour that the presence of other, abundant, large predators in a park or game reserve is unlikely to favour cheetah conservation. Lions, leopards and hyaenas scavenge freely and regularly try to purloin one another's kills. Cheetahs stand out in this respect, for they very rarely eat anything that they have not slain themselves. Thus, whereas a cheetah kill will attract other predators, cheetahs gain no return benefit through kills made by their competitors, a factor that must heighten their behavioural disadvantages. However, this reluctance to scavenge or come to carrion means that they cannot be attracted to baits and they are less vulnerable to poaching than leopards and lions.

Socially cheetahs are cat-like. Females are solitary and accompanied by males only when in oestrus, or by their dependent young. They are territorial in that they tend to stay within fixed ranges which they demarcate by urinating and defecating on or close to prominent trees, stone outcrops and the like. Males scent-mark with urine squirts in the manner of a domestic cat. They are also less solitary than females and often form lasting partnerships in which two or even three males remain together for long periods. They, too, tend to be territorial and resent intruders of the same sex into their frequently scent-marked territories. The young are born in litters of up to six, though usually less, and stay with their mothers until between eleven and twenty months old. After this they split up, females becoming independent almost immediately, brothers often staying together for longer.

Having read the available literature, we were in a position to know what to look for and to expect. Our first job was to get to know the Mara, both inside and around the peripheral areas. It meant hours of cross-country driving, and innumerable punctures. Indeed by the end of our study we were experts at changing wheels and could almost do this blindfolded. We had to replace a punctured wheel within minutes when following cheetahs as they were so easily lost in the long grass. At the outset we aimed to get to know as many of the local cheetahs as possible. Once we could identify individuals, we could then collect data on their home ranges and try to estimate how much territory the individual needed in the Mara. The first problem we had to come to terms with was learning how to find cheetahs. Being shy, they didn't display themselves readily and often hid by lying low in the grass if they saw a vehicle in their vicinity. When the grass was long they were particularly difficult to see and once we went for ten days without seeing one. To get results we had to bury our pride and watch the tourist circuits. Agglomerations of buses had to be approached to see if their focus was a cheetah; and we avidly sought information from the tour vehicle drivers and Reserve Rangers. With time, though, we became more adept at locating these animals for ourselves. We found that by driving from vantage point to vantage point, and scanning with binoculars, we could pick out cheetahs at distances of up to three kilometres (just over two miles). As our cheetah sightings mounted so the patterns of their territories became more apparent. And as we got to know where individuals were likely to be, so our chances of finding them quickly rose.

Driving about the Mara as we did, we also came to know the various grazers' reactions to predators and used them to guide us to where cheetahs might be. Raised heads all looking in one direction gave one the general area whence an alarm was coming. The topi were particularly good allies in our searches as they adopted an erect posture that was obvious from a considerable distance. Proceeding to the alarm source, we usually found a hyaena lying low in a mud hole, a lion in the shade of a bush or, if we were lucky, a cheetah. Even with the aid of binoculars and our animal sentinels, locating cheetahs was laborious. If all searches were included, we must have averaged about five hours per sighting. In contrast, the average time to locate lions was a mere seven minutes!

Having found a cheetah, we would approach it. We soon learned that a direct drive towards the animal was unproductive. The cheetah seemed to take the directness as a threat and vanished into thicker cover long before our arrival. Our normal method was to take a somewhat circular route, approaching at a tangent.

Some people have expressed surprise at the ease with which we were able to recognize individual cheetahs. To the uninitiated they appear to be spotted cats, each virtually identical to the next. And so it seemed to us at the outset. Individual cheetahs, however, are not identical. Each has different markings; some researchers use their facial spots, others the patterns of neck and chest spots, and yet another the pattern of rings on the tail, for individual identification. We used photographs of our cheetahs to check identities, though with those we saw frequently such aids were unnecessary. Just as one can recognise a pet black labrador amongst other black labradors, so one rapidly learns to identify an individual cheetah. The mind subconsciously handles all the elements of difference between individuals.

Cheetahs' reactions to motor cars differed widely. Those that were bold enough to establish territories in areas of high tourist traffic were blasé about vehicles and would tolerate as many as fifteen parked about them. They were every bit as indifferent to the watching humans as were the lions in the Mara. They hardly lifted their heads when a car approached, and would go back to sleep as soon as the ignition was switched off. Others were not so tolerant. The noise and stench of car engines and babbling tourist voices made them run for cover from which they wouldn't reappear until late evening. As cheetahs are predominantly day-time hunters, this must have reduced hunting time and influenced their way of life quite markedly.

It was not long before our two cars became well-known to the tourist drivers who operated in the Mara. And as our experience and success rate in spotting cheetahs became apparent, these drivers began to keep an eye out for us. When our vehicles stopped it was assumed that there would be a cheetah nearby and they would join us; any methodical observation was ruined. The insensitivity of these drivers, Reserve Rangers and tourists was a constant and infuriating source of disturbance. Eventually we realized that if we were to make detailed records of behaviour, there was no alternative but to spend a large proportion of our time in out-of-the-way places beyond the reach of the tour buses. Other researchers have reported the same frustrations, particularly those whose subjects have been shy. Nevertheless, such inconveniences were, in the end, a small price to pay for living and working in the Mara.

After our first year observing, we tentatively estimated that there were about fifty cheetahs resident within the Mara Reserve, and, possibly, a further fifty living in the peripheral Masai grazing lands. This was a lower figure than had previously been estimated for the area by our colleague David Burney. However, his estimates were based on taking a limited area (it later turned out that this was the one with the highest cheetah density) as representative of the whole, whereas our information derived from observation over the entire region. We accumulated our data from eight hundred hours of watching cheetahs. Some of the shyer individuals became accustomed to our vehicles and would allow us close without moving off, although if another car approached which they did not know, they would get up and leave. Initially we tried to be 'scientific' and identify them with numbers. Once we got to know some of them well, though, we gave them individual names. In the first instance we borrowed these from our map, for they gave some indication of the areas where we believed the individuals to be resident. Thus we had cheetahs called Mara, Talek and Sandy after rivers, Kurao, Musiara and Meta after Masai names for some of the plains, and Serena who lived by a lodge of that name.

In the Mara it appeared – somewhat contrary to what we had expected – that many of the cheetahs were migratory. Talek was a large male with a very distinctive tail pattern. We first saw him on 15th February 1981, moving along the river, stopping now and then to spray urine on tree trunks as his *imprimatur*. We saw him on five more occasions before the end of March as far as eight kilometres from the river. He then disappeared completely and we didn't see him again until January 12th 1982 when he arrived back in his original hunting grounds. Where had he been in the meantime? And so it was with all other males we came to know in the Mara. None of them stayed put in any area for more than two months at a time. Once, two male cheetahs who were very tame arrived on the scene. Their tameness was strange, for this normally only develops through constant association with vehicles and humans. As they were unknown to all Mara residents, including ourselves, where had they come from? The most reasonable suggestion was from Seronera in the Serengeti, 112 kilometres (70 miles) away to the south. They then disappeared as suddenly as they had arrived, and we never did find out their secret.

As expected, with the females it was different. While some were more mobile than we first thought would be the case, they did seem more sedentary. But in our long hours and weeks spent observing cheetahs, we were able to monitor only one mother and her three cubs continuously over a span of fifteen months. They gave us a clear idea of the size of their home range; it comprised one hundred square kilometres (about 40 square miles).

Our activities followed a set routine. We would rise with the sun at about 6.30 a.m. and be off looking for cheetahs after a cup of tea. We would search all parts of the Reserve and also covered large areas of the surrounding Masailand. Around the middle of the day we might refresh ourselves with a picnic snack as we watched cheetahs or other wildlife. The Reserve rules forbade night-driving and we would be back in camp by 7 p.m. After a bath we would clean our equipment and write up our diaries, before having our one hot meal of the day. By 8.30 p.m. we would have turned in and blown out the lights.

The schedule was naturally subject to the vehicles being in running order. Constant off-road driving took its toll and, perforce, we had to carry out our own time-consuming repairs. And of course there were times when our routines were unavoidably upset. Trying to follow cheetahs often meant crossing streams or seasonal water courses (luggahs) and, inevitably, there was the occasional misjudgment. One such incident saw our wheels sink so deep into mud that we could not drive or dig our way out. Karl had no option but to walk for help to the nearest tourist camp. Providing that one is alert, walking among wild animals is not the perilous undertaking that Hollywood would have us believe. The Masai do it daily with as little concern as the Londoner moving down his urban streets. On the way back to the stranded car, Karl discovered he had earlier walked within a few paces of twelve lions without seeing them. They had lain low as he passed and, as his unconcern was no different from what they were accustomed to from the Masai, done nothing. Had Karl seen the lions at close range and reacted with shock, he might have triggered a different and more unpleasant response. It is the unexpected that so often stimulates a predator to investigate.

We had other encounters with lions. Once a camera fell out of the car, close to a pride we were photographing. To our consternation a young male came over and picked it up. We drove after him and he dropped it. Fortunately it was intact though coated in saliva and smelled strongly of lion. There was a group of young lions that had an inconvenient hobby of demolishing campers' lavatory tents. Why this happened we never established. Maybe the smell of urine in their territory caught their attention? They did, however, leave our 'little house' alone, perhaps because the wood ash we used in it effectively masked other smells.

Occasionally we took a break to replenish our stores from one of the tourist lodges, or from Nairobi. When heavy rains fell we stayed in camp, for the Mara's black-cotton soil becomes a morass that no vehicle can cross. Thus day followed day and the months passed. Life was simple, and this simplicity was a large part of its attraction. Involved as we were in our cheetah watching, we never really missed the amenities of civilization.

Like many cat species, cheetahs are largely solitary.
However, they communicate their presence to their fellows
by depositing scent. Here a cheetah sniffs a marking post
for the latest 'bulletin' and then adds his own message. As
with the domestic tom cat, this is done with a backward
squirt of urine – tail held high.

Below, opposite and overleaf: No two cheetahs are identical. Each has its own spot pattern, just as humans have individual fingerprints. Some have broad faces, others narrow and such characteristics make the individual easy to recognize.

Below and overleaf: A gazelle's eye view of a stalking cheetah: well camouflaged by the long grass, it is easy to appreciate why the hunter is difficult to see until too close.

Below: A reversal of roles; the viewer viewed. Sandy, one of our favourite cheetahs, watches a wheel change.

Overleaf: Cheetahs are largely diurnal. A family tends to spend the night in one spot as, in this case, has Mara and her cubs. At sunrise they wake and the hunter's day begins.

# 3 · The Hunter's Day

Cheetahs are the most diurnal of all the great cats. Though they occasionally move about after dark, the night is usually spent in a small area and for the most part, resting. This is particularly so with families and we found that we could generally find a mother and cubs at dawn in the same place that we had left them the evening before. A daily routine depends to a degree upon how recently the individual has fed. Like many large predators, the species engorges after a large kill and can then go for several days without a major meal. The hungry cheetah starts seeking prey soon after dawn. Stretching and yawning around first light, it gazes about, characteristically sitting on its haunches. If it sees nothing in the vicinity of the night's resting place, the cheetah may proceed to a vantage point, a high termite mound or a low branch (which it will, in all probability, mark with urine), and again stare and stare about it. Thus a patrol from one lookout point to another begins until a victim is sighted and hunted, or until the sun becomes too hot, usually after 9.30 a.m.

With rising temperature the cheetah finds its urge to hunt conflicting more and more with a desire to seek shade. Eventually an attractive resting place is reached and the patrol is over for the morning. Such a site is often a patch of shade on the fringe of some bushes or under a tree. Almost invariably the position offers a good field of view in at least one direction. As the sun climbs higher the cheetah sleeps in numerous cat-like positions: on its back, on its belly, using available supports as props and pillows, but usually flat on its side. From time to time, whatever its pose, it raises its head and stares down its field of view. If some unsuspecting victim comes to within hunting range, the cheetah is alert in a trice. If the situation then develops favourably it may attempt a kill, regardless of the time.

If the heat of the day passes uneventfully, the dropping temperature of afternoon again brings the cheetah to its feet and, as in the morning, it sets off on patrol. This may continue until a meal has been secured or night falls, when the animal beds down again.

The daily routine of a full bellied cheetah is similar, if less energetic. There are patrols during the early and late cool hours, with much sniffing and scent marking at prominent posts, and long hot-hour siestas.

The cheetah's hunting technique shows several variations upon a central theme. That theme is a stalk, followed by a chase at high speed, seizure of the victim's throat and its strangulation. The enormous exertion of a high speed chase builds up a huge oxygen deficiency in the victim's system. In this condition its death is very rapid when the cheetah clamps off its windpipe. It simply does not have the resources left to put up a violent struggle. It is because of this highly specialized technique that cheetahs do not need the huge muscular strength of the other big cats, which do not deliberately build up an oxygen deficiency before closing with their victims. Instead they seize quarry after a close stalk and very short rush or pounce, when it still has abundant reserves for struggle. Thus lions, leopards, tigers and jaguars need great strength to subdue large victims, huge, curved claws to hold them and powerful jaws with long canines with which to bite and stab vital organs deep inside the body.

The chase seems so important to the cheetah hunting technique that, if for some reason the prey remains stationary upon the predator's approach, the hunt is usually abandoned. We witnessed a classic illustration of this. A female cheetah was clearly fascinated by something nearby. Driving closer we saw that she was watching a male impala some twenty paces distant. It was alive, but badly wounded by poachers. We retreated to watch from a distance.

The cheetah slowly approached the antelope with every indication of wishing to capture it. The impala could see the cheetah coming and tried on several occasions to get to its feet but couldn't, and seemingly because of this failure to play its expected flight role, the cheetah came no closer than ten paces to it. Although the cat was slack-bellied and obviously could have done with a feed, it never moved in for the kill. Eventually, after closely watching the impala for an hour, the cheetah went away, presumably looking for a victim that would act in the conventional manner. Other observers have reported similar incidents in which cheetahs have approached quarry which did not run, but stood staring back or snorting. In each instance the cheetah abandoned the hunt.

Late in 1981 we spent many days with Sandy, a female who at the time had five small cubs. We accompanied her on all her hunts and watched her employ three variations of the cheetah hunting theme:

On November 25th Sandy leaves her cubs at approximately 7.30 a.m. and begins a hunting patrol. Moving along a ridge in the cover of light bush, she skirts and searches an area of open grassland. After three-quarters of an hour she sights five Thomson's gazelles grazing about sixty paces from her. Sandy immediately commences a stalk. The initial approach is straightforward — a few quick steps towards them using the cover of the fringing bushes. There is, however, still a gap of some forty paces between her and the gazelles in which there's no cover, other than the long but wispy grass. After watching the gazelles for several minutes, the cheetah emerges from behind the last bush; head low, in a semi-crouch, staring intently at the quarry, she moves forward slowly. Whenever a gazelle looks up, Sandy freezes into immobility. As soon as their heads are down, the stalk continues until the distance between predator and prey is down to thirty paces. At that point the cheetah sinks, head almost on the ground. Something, probably scent, alarms the gazelles and their heads come up. One of them takes several swift steps and the cheetah rises and moves with trotting steps towards the 'tommies'. Seeing her, they scatter. It seems as though it's not until they have commenced their flight that she decides which one to go for. The indecision is over: the smallest gazelle breaks to the left and the cheetah focuses on it. Sandy's trot accelerates and almost immediately she is travelling as only a cheetah after its prey can — the fastest mammal on earth. The long, supple back hunches and stretches rhythmically as the fore and hind limbs come together and part in long, low bounds. In less than twenty paces Sandy is upon the gazelle and it clearly has no chance against her superior speed in straight flight. But just as the cheetah is upon it, the gazelle jinks left, then right and what has been a clear run now becomes a crazy zigzag course. The cat tries to follow each move, turning this way and that, with the long cheetah tail serving as a counterbalance in the turns. The distance between hunter and hunted widens and it seems as though the gazelle's dodging is paying off. It corners round a small mound, but Sandy has anticipated the move and comes over the top of the obstacle. Her paw flashes out with blunt claws spread, cat-like, to hit the gazelle's hindquarters. It tumbles and there is a cloud of dust in which Sandy sits with her jaws clamped about the victim's throat and her body well clear of the now weakly kicking hooves. She holds this position for one and three-quarter minutes before letting go. The gazelle moves slightly and she resumes her throat-hold for another minute. The cheetah is breathing at one hundred and fifty breaths a minute and it takes her twenty-five minutes before she recovers sufficiently to take the kill into cover and commence feeding. In typical cheetah fashion she starts at the rump.

Two days later Sandy is back in the same place. This time she lies behind a bush on a low ant-hill watching another group of Thomson's gazelle. They are unaware of her presence and graze towards her. As they approach she crouches close to the ground and watches. Closer and closer, and though the leading gazelle frequently raises its head and looks straight at Sandy, her immobility is an effective camouflage. Eventually when a gazelle comes to within two paces, the cheetah moves. The gazelle jumps, twisting away from her into flight, but it never comes to a chase for the cheetah is on it in mid-air and when they hit the ground together, Sandy already has her death clamp about its throat. On this occasion the hunt is almost a 'conventional' cat-type hunt: stealthy, with a very short rush.

Very young Thomson's gazelles spend much of their time lying motionless amongst clumps of grass. When danger threatens a standing herd, they drop to the ground while adults leave them and flee. In an area where these gazelles are abundant, such as the Mara, cheetahs learn that a little patient searching may turn up a motionless fawn. We have watched cheetahs quartering an area, working backwards and forwards, taking no notice of adult gazelles nearby. More often than not they are successful in their search and snatch the youngster off the ground or seize it after only a few paces. Sometimes, though, they fail and, involved as we were with our cheetahs and their welfare, it always gladdened us to see a baby 'tommy' appear, seemingly from nowhere, once the cheetahs had gone. On 12th December 1981 we watch Sandy's third variation as she crosses an open plain. Without warning she breaks into a canter and moves into top speed, apparently for no reason. When we come up with her forty seconds and two hundred and fifty paces later, she is carrying a baby 'tommy' to a shady spot to rest and feed. She obviously saw the fawn in the same instant that it saw her and crouched, and she had gone directly to the spot.

Cheetahs catch African hares in much the same manner as gazelle fawns. These animals are given to lying throughout the day under bushes and among grass clumps. Waiting until the last minute they burst out of cover with white-flashing scut to startle a human, or become easy meat for a cheetah. With such small animals cheetahs kill with a bite through head and neck.

While Thomson's gazelles seemed to be the favourite quarry in the Mara, the written records indicate that cheetahs take a wide range of animals as prey. The list includes rats, game birds, small antelopes such as dik-dik, duikers, oribis, impala and reed buck, more rarely large species including a roan antelope, a young giraffe, young buffaloes, zebras, wildebeests, and both warthogs and aardvarks. Generally the large animals are only tackled by several cheetahs hunting together. When alone they do not often take animals weighing over sixty kilos (130 lb).

From our observations we confirmed that cheetahs in the Mara region are efficient hunters, have a lower failure rate than lions and hyaenas, and are only exceeded in competence by the wild dog. Nevertheless we did witness an occasional mishap. On August 12th 1981 we had spent most of the day with a large male cheetah. In the late afternoon he moved out onto a plain where there were several groups of wildebeests. Clearly he was interested and made two rather half-hearted unsuccessful rushes at them in an endeavour to separate a young calf from its herd. After the second try he hid in a clump of bush where he stayed for about three-quarters of an hour. The wildebeests seemed to have forgotten about him when he emerged and ran towards a group at nearly top speed. It had the right effect, for the wildebeests fled. Their path was obstructed by a small, stony hill which made them spread out in line. The cheetah focused on the last of them, a youngish calf, and after a classic run, tripped it with a blow to the hindquarters and fastened on its throat. (While on occasions the blow to the hindquarters appears to be a swipe that trips the victim, many of the kills we examined showed a deep claw-scratch on the rump inflicted by the cheetah's dew-claw. This, the most curved and cat-like of all its claws, it apparently uses as a hook to upset its prey.) We were still driving up toward the kill when a group of wildebeests returned to the scene. Several adults charged at the cheetah who let his victim go and fled, pursued by his erstwhile victims.

On another occasion we were following a cheetah family consisting of a female with three almost fully grown cubs. A group of five topis were also on the same plain. One of the young cheetahs who was somewhat behind the rest decided to test the topis and cantered at them. Presumably if they had done what was expected of them, a full chase might have developed. But the expected did not happen. The topis, who had been watching the cheetah all along, were not taken by surprise and, as one, charged the astonished predators, who fled. The chase went on over at least three hundred metres and ended ignominiously with two of the cheetahs hiding six feet up in a bush, looking scared and uncomfortable.

Predation confronted us with a paradox. Emotionally we always felt sorry for the victim. Kathrine, in particular, was upset by death in all its forms. Indeed, once her feelings nearly got her into trouble. Driving towards four cheetahs across open grassland, she flushed a gazelle fawn from where it lay crouching unseen. Away went the baby straight toward the cheetahs. Kathy felt terrible and utterly responsible for the poor mite's life. The cheetahs caught the fawn, but it managed to get away, badly mauled. In its terror it fled back to our vehicle, the cheetahs close behind. It arrived alongside and without thought Kathrine leapt out to gather it in her arms — bringing four amazed cheetahs to skidding halts only two or three paces off. At that point, however, discipline took over and she let the event run its course by getting back into the car. The incident hurt her deeply.

Why we felt distressed by kills we don't know, for it is all part and parcel of the natural scene which so attracted us. Such attitudes may be somewhat peculiar to our generation for the literature of our grandfathers' times seems to exult in 'grand' death and exhibits little sympathy for the victims of either predators or sportsmen (except of course when the predator stole the victim from the sportsman!). Perhaps our emotions have been set by the violence of the modern world and the seemingly endless bloodshed. But no matter how much we emotionally identified with our cheetahs' victims and the sadness of a fawn's end, we observed no more magnificent a sight than the spotted one, hurling itself on a victim at seventy miles an hour, every bit nature's epitome of speed and symmetry, agility and grace.

In the manner of all waking cats, the roused cheetah
stretches and stretches again.

Opposite: Having toned its muscles through stretching, the hunter climbs a vantage point in search of prey.

Below: The quarry is slowly stalked to within forty paces.

Overleaf: Mara and her family have just seen a victim as indicated by the lowered heads of the two leading animals. This signals the start of a stalk, throughout which the head will not be raised above the stalker's general back line. The two at the rear have not yet recognized their mother's intentions and thus are likely to spoil the hunt.

As soon as the victim sees the cheetah and starts to flee, the predator breaks into a run. Within a few bounds it is at top speed. The two extreme positions here illustrate both cheetah suppleness and the great length of stride.

Overleaf: The chase, usually over several hundred metres, builds up a huge oxygen deficiency in the victim. Here, the victim's gasping mouth, illustrates this condition as the cheetah closes in.

Occasionally, as in this photograph, a cheetah might
ambush its quarry.

Sometimes with a small victim, the cheetah strangles it
while walking back to cover.

The kill is made to a set formula: the fleeing prey is knocked, tripped or hooked off balance with a blow from the cheetah's forepaw, and its throat seized. With windpipe clamped shut and desperately short of oxygen, the victim hasn't the reserves to struggle much and dies quickly. Mara demonstrates the stranglehold on a female impala.

Unlike lions, families of cheetahs arrange themselves in a
star formation around their kill to give each access to part
of it, and they consume it without much noisy quarrelling.

After a family feed individuals help clean one another of gore. Here Mara is cleaned by one of her sons.

Opposite: Towards the end of the hunters' day the scavengers move in.

Overleaf: A family watch intently. Their raised heads indicate that it is a source of curiosity or possible alarm. Had it been a potential victim for them, they would have lowered their heads. The immature neck mane stands out clearly on one of the cubs.

It was an important aspect of our study to record how cheetahs reacted to other animals and *vice versa*, particularly in view of their timidity. From the observations of other research workers there was an idea about that cheetah conservation might not be best served by those parks in which other large predators were abundant. Any information we could bring to bear on this subject would be valuable.

For first-hand evidence on cheetahs and monkeys we had Nuggy, a small vervet given to us by the animal orphanage in Nairobi for re-introduction and eventual release into the wild. From the time of her arrival in the Mara, Nuggy was the spirit of our camp. Lively, playful and forever curious, this gentle little animal quickly won our hearts. She often accompanied us cheetah watching and her antics helped us while away the long, actionless hours that are a feature of many predator studies. Nuggy accustomed herself to our dangerous (in a monkey's eyes) habit of driving close to carnivores that instinct told her were unfriendly. However, cheetahs were often fascinated by the nimble little creature behind the car's glass windows. From the way that they behaved, the close approaches and hard stares, we had little doubt that they saw her as potential prey. Their reactions also disproved the belief that animals outside a vehicle cannot recognize others inside it. If cheetahs could see that Nuggy was potential prey, then by the same argument they must have realized that the humans inside were not part of the furnishings!

The manner in which cheetahs bolt their food, constantly looking about them, suggests fear that they may be robbed of their quarry. This is understandable for lions, leopards, hyaenas and jackals are all as much scavengers as they are killers. They keep a constant lookout for signs of death and follow them up whenever they occur. They watch vultures, as a concentration of these birds circling over a dead animal and their steep descents on to one, are signposts that can be seen over great distances. Being professional opportunists, lions and hyaenas often drive each other from kills, let alone so submissive an animal as the cheetah. A common cheetah reaction upon sighting lions, leopards and hyaenas is slinking away, head held low. Though we never witnessed such a case ourselves, there have been instances in which both lions and leopards have killed and eaten cheetahs as though they were just another herbivore. On a recent sad instance in the Serengeti, some tourists persuaded their driver to chase a cheetah with their car to see how fast it ran. They harried it over a long distance, unaware that the animal is a sprinter capable of high speeds over only short distances. Further, it seems that cheetahs can achieve their maximum speed only when chasing quarry and not when running defensively. Alack, when the cheetah was on the point of exhaustion it was driven accidentally onto a pride of resting lions. With no reserves left it could not get away and the lions killed it.

Later in this book we recount an instance in which lions killed a litter of cheetah cubs. Yet it would appear that other predators do this as well. Once we came upon a female cheetah that was obviously on edge. She stared toward a tree stump – seemingly wanting to go to it, but frightened to do so. Eventually she did walk over, pick something up in her mouth and walk away. Though we couldn't see what it was that she carried, we managed to take a photograph before she dropped the object. After a fruitless search in the long grass for whatever it was, we went to the tree stump and found the remains of three small cubs. From the bite marks they had apparently been killed by a small predator, we assumed a jackal or a pair of them. Later, when our film was developed, it transpired that the object dropped by the female cheetah had been a fourth dead cub.

We watched two lionesses chase our female, Sandy, from a tommy that she had just killed. There are instances elsewhere in which cheetahs have been seen abandoning kills, not only to big predators, but to animals smaller than themselves such as jackals and even vultures. In the Mara, jackals were very disrespectful towards cheetahs, yapping at and harrying them virtually whenever their paths crossed. From what we saw, therefore, we believe that the presence of other large predators in any numbers is not conducive to cheetah well-being.

It is not only carnivores that bring out cheetah timidity. Baboons, ruffians of the bush that they may be, have no apparent reason to either fear or molest the gentle cats. Yet, on several occasions we watched a troop go out of their way to chase cheetahs. Perhaps they felt that because of the spotted coats, they were indirectly getting back at a cat that baboons have rather more respect for – the leopard!

One day a large warthog appeared as we watched a cheetah at siesta under a bush. The hog, too, obviously thought that it would like to rest there. Without ado it walked straight at the cheetah, which fled, ignominiously abandoning its bed to the pig.

Yet, from time to time, the worm turns. While spotted hyaenas normally drive cheetahs off kills with impunity, we saw a female cheetah turn on a single hyaena, chase it and bite it severely in the back. The Frames, who studied cheetahs in the nearby Serengeti, watched a female cheetah that had cubs charge an approaching lioness and put it to flight. On another occasion we were following one of our better known females, Mara, and her three large cubs, when they came across a solitary lion. The cubs surrounded the lion and closed in towards him. When they were within twenty paces, the astonished lion charged one of the cubs which fled, easily keeping away from its pursuer. When the lion stopped the cubs repeated their performance and kept up their teasing until dark fell. Throughout, Mara sat well aside and watched the game with apparent unconcern!

The Frames saw a similar event in which the victim was a rhino which young cheetahs tormented for ten minutes or so before tiring of the game. Apart from this instance, however, neutrality or indifference seems to prevail between cheetahs and the larger herbivora. Giraffes will follow cheetahs out of curiosity, but we never saw much interaction between the two species. Elephants, which take a most unfriendly interest in the close proximity of lions, were utterly unconcerned about cheetahs. Even when the cats were well within the pachyderms' sight, they gave little indication of being bothered by the cheetahs' presence.

The elephants' tolerance was particularly notable once when we were watching the female, Sandy, who had a litter of small cubs hidden in a clump of bushes. A herd of elephants approached and were soon browsing all about Sandy's lair. She sat in the open nearby and we had no doubt that both elephants and cheetah were aware of each other. The female cheetah showed no concern until a young elephant went to within five paces of where the cubs were hidden. At that, the cheetah jumped up and hissed vehemently at the intruder, who rapidly backed away.

Opposite top: Nuggy, our tame vervet monkey, notes the unusual form of human teeth and tries to figure out what happened to that last bite of banana.

Opposite bottom: Nuggy sometimes accompanied us cheetah watching. Cheetahs were fascinated by the monkey and showed quite clearly that they could recognize animate objects inside a car.

81

Giraffes are unafraid of cheetahs and often follow them out of curiosity, but elephants and cheetahs largely ignore one another.

Cheetahs usually run away from lions, leopards and hyaenas. On this unusual occasion the tormented turns tormentor and a female cheetah sets about a single hyaena, dusting his backside thoroughly.

Jackals show scant respect for cheetahs. With the migration in the background giving this cheetah a wide berth, a jackal impertinently sniffs at the big cat's tail.

Overleaf: Typically cat-like, cheetah courtship is turbulent. Here a female in oestrus abuses an ardent suitor who is so strongly attracted by her tantalising scents that he must sniff every place she stopped.

Kipling's tale of the cat that walked by itself highlights a cornerstone of feline behaviour generally. Cats, with a very few exceptions like lions, are solitary animals. Most keep clear of their own kind except to mate or when a female has dependent young. They keep 'tabs' on one another and advertise presence to their fellows by scent, a common feature of which is the deposition of urine and dung on certain sites. Whereas male dogs cock a leg with flamboyant insouciance, the domestic tom cat illustrates the feline style: backing up to the 'marker post' and letting fly a rearward jet of urine, simultaneously treading the rear feet and wriggling the vertically held tail. By performing in a similar manner, male cheetahs show themselves to be very much cats in this aspect of behaviour.

Many cats, and especially the bigger species, reinforce olfactory messages with loud sound. While the noises made may be intended primarily for communication within their own societies, they are also striking features of the general environment and are heard and recognized by other species. Cheetahs, rather in keeping with their inoffensive natures, are exceptions to this. They do not roar and their calls are not prominent aural features of the lands in which they live. Nevertheless, as befits their status as cats, they do have quite a wide repertoire of sounds. Like domestic cats they purr when contented, though on a scale in keeping with their larger size. Such purring is heard when mother greets and grooms her young and a louder, more staccato version is characteristic when a male courts a female. Cheetahs also growl warnings both to other cheetahs and other animals and they hiss and spit explosively in defence. They also have some calls that are uniquely their own. Both mother and young make a curious bird-like chirp when trying to keep in contact with one another. It is difficult to equate this sound with a large predatory cat. As they become older and have growing need to communicate over greater distances, this chirping evolves into an explosive yelp. Again, while it carries for a considerable distance, the noise is surprisingly 'small' for animals of this size. It is used when adults call to one another or when a female is trying to locate lost cubs and her normal cub-call, a churring sound, has failed.

Over ninety per cent of our cheetah sightings in and about the Mara were of single animals, a fact that stresses the species' generally solitary mode of life. This lack of sociability is particularly a feature of females. We never saw two adult female cheetahs together. However, some males go about in pairs and sometimes trios. In many instances these adult male partnerships are suspected of being brothers out of the same litter of cubs.

Even immature cheetahs seem to be hostile towards others from outside their families. Thus a young animal that was playing beside our vehicle caught sight of itself in the highly polished car door. After inspecting the image briefly it spat and struck the ground with both front paws in aggressive display. Having done this twice, it moved away quickly.

While we never saw adult female cheetahs consorting, we were present once when two saw one another. We parked to watch a female called Tana who lay on a small anthill with her single, almost fully grown male cub. Every now and then the young male would stare in our direction, seemingly not at, but past us. Eventually we followed his gaze and there, not twenty paces away was a strange cheetah. The scene was laid for an interesting contact and we drew back a little way so as not to interfere. Suspecting that the stranger might be a male interested in Tana we hoped to witness the hitherto elusive sequences of mating behaviour. Female cheetahs usually come on heat about the time that their young are full grown and this was precisely Tana's situation.

Nothing happened until evening when the stranger stood up. To our disappointment it was a female. Tana watched and her son became very alert. The stranger left the shade in which she had been lying and walked toward the other pair. At some fifteen paces distance the young male lowered his head and growled. The strange female immediately changed direction and slunk away in a crouching posture that we had previously only seen when cheetahs encountered other predator species. Similar avoiding behaviour has been observed elsewhere. Thus even though female cheetahs sometimes hunt across the same grounds and, on occasion, have litters within a few hundred metres of each other, they rigorously avoid direct contact and association.

In all our time in the Mara we witnessed no encounters between male cheetah strangers. Those that we saw together were obviously members of established partnerships. From the Serengeti, however, we know that while some males are nomads, others establish territories from which they eject strange males. On occasion, when a partnership of resident males has combined against intruders, ejections have ended fatally. However, the area in which these observations were made held a higher density of cheetahs than occurred in the Mara and, we suspect that as such violence is related to high density, then it may be rare in the area we studied.

When a female cheetah comes into oestrus this is signalled to others through her scent. A male crossing her paths receives the information and follows her. The literature indicates that the affair is typically feline. The male seems torn between avoiding the normally solitary female and the enticements of the messages she leaves. He approaches calling and purring in alternation. For her part, the female also seems divided between repelling an intruder and accepting his close presence. This conflict was apparent in the only courtship behaviour that we saw. One morning we came across two cheetahs lying a few feet apart in long grass. One was male and the other female, and both were strangers to us. In the next twenty minutes the male approached the female from behind on three occasions and on each she rose up on her hind legs and slapped at him with her forepaws. After each rebuff he retreated and lay down again. As is so often the case when an event of exceptional interest takes place, we had left our video camera in camp. We rushed and were back with the cheetahs within twenty minutes, to spend the rest of the day with them.

Soon after we returned the two cheetahs separated by some thirty paces and slept until 5.30 in the evening. Awakening, the female walked past where the male lay, giving a quick purr as she passed him. He roused himself and followed her closely to a pool in the bottom of a nearby luggah where they drank. From then until dusk they played like cubs, repeatedly climbing up and jumping down the steep banks. At dusk they retraced their earlier steps and we left them near where we had found them that morning.

The following day we were up early and back to where we had left our couple. The male was there, but the female was nowhere to be seen. The erstwhile suitor seemed distraught and seemed to be searching for the female among the nearby clumps of bush and thicket. Eventually he climbed an anthill and stared about him until the heat of the sun drove him to shelter and sleep in deep shade. We saw him no more after that.

Two days later, however, we came across the female who was by herself. Frequently she stopped her patrol and yelped, but no male appeared. There were no indications that she had cubs in the vicinity or had recently suckled any and we assumed that she was calling for a mate, presumably because she was now ready. Though we kept the area under observation it was to no avail. Frustratingly we never saw another courtship and we were never able to photograph this aspect of cheetah behaviour. The nearest we got was a mock mating between two immatures in the same litter, when an adolescent male mounted his sister without serious intent. However it did, if nothing else, illustrate that the mounting male grasps the female's nape in his jaws: again, very cat-like behaviour.

Opposite: The female in the previous picture was not quite ready for mating. Her suitor left her, but two days later we found her yelping continuously, presumably now ready to mate and advertising the fact.

Cheetahs mating: in this instance a mock performance
between two immatures from the same family. However, it
nevertheless illustrates the male grasp of the female nape –
typically feline.

The outcome of courtship: Mara, heavily pregnant.

Overleaf: Mother and young – Sandy with her one-month-old cubs.

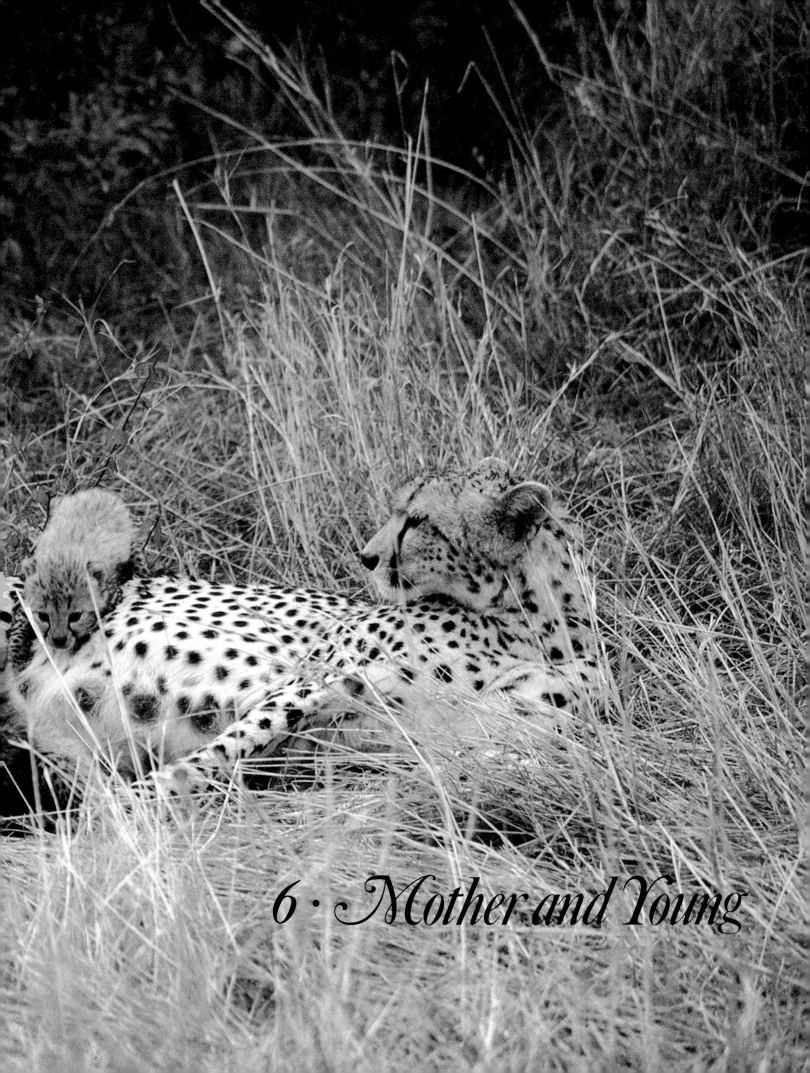

*6 · Mother and Young*

Among the most interesting aspects of any wildlife study are those concerning the birth and growth of the young. Following cheetah families' progress provided the most emotionally rewarding of our Mara experiences.

Through October 1981 we kept a watchful eye on Sandy who was heavily pregnant. She would be an ideal mother to follow for she was tame and allowed us to approach her closely. However, keeping track of her was easier said than done. In mid-November we lost touch and spent several unsuccessful days trying to find her. Returning home one evening, rather despondently, we bumped into her quite by accident. She was no longer pregnant. She walked along a luggah amongst scattered bush and we followed slowly. Eventually she arrived at a thicket into which she disappeared, after much sniffing of the ground and staring about her. Dark was now falling and we returned to camp.

The next morning, November 23rd, we returned at sunrise and drove right up to the bush into which Sandy had disappeared the evening before. Peering through the leaves and branches we could see her indistinct outline. Satisfied that she hadn't slipped away during the night, we drew back to watch and wait. At seven-thirty Sandy's head appeared through her lair's leafy screen and a moment later she bounded out into the open. After yawning and stretching she made her way to an anthill, looked about, defecated and set off through the surrounding high grass. We were in a dilemma. Should we follow her or should we take the opportunity of her absence to confirm that she had cubs and take a close look at them? We followed Sandy.

She was obviously hungry and hunting, but it took her until after ten in the morning to find and catch a tommy. This kill didn't attract any scavengers and we felt that there were unlikely to be any interesting developments about it. Taking advantage of the cheetah's preoccupation with her meal, we returned to the lair to examine her cubs. There they were, five small balls of black fluff huddled together. Their eyes were still tightly closed and they appeared to us to be, at most, four to five days old. Cheetah cubs are born with an unusual colour pattern, being a rather dirty white above and black below. The black soon starts to disappear and is replaced with the familiar spots on a pale background. The white upper parts develop into a mantle of long greyish hair and this in turn slowly gives way to the adult colouring. By three months the mantle has been shed except on the top of the shoulders and neck, where it appears as a somewhat wispy mane. This is eventually lost altogether, though even at fifteen months vestiges are present.

Having examined Sandy's cubs we withdrew and watched. We didn't have long to wait before she returned and plunged into the thicket to suckle her young. For the next twenty-five days we spent an average of ten rewarding hours a day with Sandy's family. The mother developed a predictable routine. She left the lair between seven-twenty and eight-forty-five, stretched, looked about, defecated and then set off on patrol. This usually proceeded along a ridge that ran close to the luggah in which she located her lair. When hungry she devoted her time to hunting but, if well fed the previous day, she merely strolled about her range. Usually she was back with her litter well before noon. Upon arrival the cubs scrambled to get at her teats, but after the initial energies had been expended, the rest of the day passed quietly.

Sandy moved the cubs to new lairs every four days or so. Before they could walk she would pick them up and, holding them by the scruff of their necks, carry them one by one to a new site. The first move was to another bush only five paces from the first lair. The second was a bigger project. Returning from patrol one morning she didn't join the cubs but walked along the luggah for about two hundred paces, inspecting each clump of bush that she came to. Having done this she returned to the lair and suckled the cubs. Shortly after one o'clock she emerged carrying a cub by the scruff of its neck and took it to one of the clumps she had inspected previously. The process was repeated four times. Some cubs were easier to carry than others. The third she kept putting down, trying to get a better grip and, to our consternation, she carried the fifth by one front leg! The new site was not very comfortable for the afternoon sun beat into it. Sandy removed herself to shade under another bush near by. The cubs responded to their discomfort by crawling in all directions. Sandy saw this, came over, picked them up and replaced them on the spot of her choice. Later, however, she did move them to another more protective shrub.

We think that the frequent moves Sandy made will have prevented the build-up of a strong cheetah smell that might help hyaenas and other scavengers to locate the cubs. At times she had trouble counting! On at least one occasion she returned to a lair plainly searching for a cub after she had already moved all five to a new site.

Fourteen days after we had found Sandy's cubs, all had opened their eyes. However, their irises were matt grey and they didn't seem to see very well. About this time we twice took advantage of Sandy's absence on a hunt to have close looks at the cubs. On both occasions the cubs spat when they heard the strange noise of our approach. They did not necessarily spit directly at us, and it seemed that while they were aware of intruding presences, they couldn't visually identify them.

At three weeks the cubs could crawl and, albeit unsteadily and with frequent hindquarter collapses, they could stand. Twenty-five days after we discovered the cubs, Sandy took them on their first walk. Returning from a hunt early one afternoon, she stopped some way from the lair. After a careful look about her, she called to her cubs. The sound was reminiscent of a bird call – a single modulated note repeated with varying intensity. Immediately a cub emerged from under a bush and toddled towards Sandy. Within two minutes all five were in the open, making their shaky way to her, or rather to where they thought she was. Each had different ideas on this and soon all five were headed in different directions. All were giving their own little chirrups, confusing both themselves and their mother. One headed for our car which, tolerant of us as she was, Sandy did not like. She rushed over, grabbed it by the scruff and moved it further away. After considerable problems, for the cubs were now too big for her to carry easily, she managed to collect them under the bush that was to be their new lair. When all were united Sandy lay in their midst purring loudly and no doubt in relief at having overcome the problems of the litter's first walk.

A week prior to the first walk we witnessed an incident that we have not seen referred to in the literature on cheetahs. Sandy had a successful morning hunt and killed a young tommy. We left her to refuel our car and anticipated finding her with the cubs on our return. Surprisingly she had not joined them and we went back to where she had killed. Nearby we came across a lioness in the open, which was unusual as the sun was still high and hot. And then we saw Sandy sitting in the shade of a tree stump only forty paces away. To our amazement Sandy stood up and walked towards the lioness who folded back her ears, growled and charged the cheetah. Sandy had no problem staying ahead of her pursuer who covered a mere twenty paces or so. Only after the performance had been repeated for the third time did we suspect a reason for it. On each occasion the cheetah had led the lioness in the same direction, and it was directly away from her cubs. Was this a deliberate attempt to remove the lioness from the proximity of her family? We think so and had we been able to watch the deadly game a little longer we may have become more certain about it. Unfortunately a tourist vehicle saw that we had stopped and came to share whatever it was that we were looking at. And in the ignorance that we found so infuriating, it parked directly between the two cats – the better to see them both! Of course that was the end of the interaction.

On December 18th Karl developed severe chest pains and we flew to Nairobi for diagnosis and treatment. Fortunately the condition, brought about through hours sitting in a certain position while bumping across rough terrain, was not serious. We returned to the Mara on the following day to resume our sojourn with Sandy and her cubs. While we were away a friend had agreed to keep an eye on the cheetahs for us and to keep up the flow of information. When he arrived at the latest lair, our friend found a pride of lions feeding on a zebra that they had killed within fifty paces of the cubs. When he left as dusk fell, Sandy was watching them from a short distance away. Our friend returned early the next morning to a sad sight. Sandy was carrying a dead cub up the ridge away from the luggah. He went immediately to the lair where there were three more dead cubs. The fifth could not be found.

Receiving the news on our return from the city, we rushed to the scene. When we investigated on foot it was apparent that the cubs had been killed by lions on the previous evening, most likely by the pride that had been eating the zebra nearby. We were sickened and upset. This family that had come to mean so much to us personally and to our study, had met with such a seemingly pointless end. Hoping that Sandy might have saved the fifth cub, we set out to find her. We found her about one and a half kilometres (about one mile) away in the shade of an acacia tree. She was distinctly on edge and jumped several times in reaction to slight noises nearby. As evening drew down she left the shade and headed back to the last lair. Our hopes rose. Did she know where the missing fifth cub was? But other than to sniff around bushes near the lair, she did nothing. Eventually we left her sitting on her haunches, staring towards the dead cubs. When she was still there the next morning we became certain that the fifth cub, too, must be dead. Sandy stayed in the area for the rest of the day, occasionally moaning with a low 'uuuu'. We had heard this call previously only from cheetahs that felt threatened by lions or leopards. Two days later Sandy disappeared and we never saw her again during our study.

Opposite top: Two-day-old cheetahs hidden in a thicket. In
their mother's absence they huddle for warmth.
Opposite bottom: Even before their eyes are open,
newborn cheetahs will hiss at any disturbance.

Eyes newly opened and greyish in colour, baby cheetahs stare at the world.

Opposite: Every few days the mother moves her cubs to a new lair, carrying them if needs be.

Below and opposite: Soon after their eyes open the cubs start to play among themselves and with their mother. This is Serena with six-week-old youngsters. Once mobile they follow their mother and expect her undivided attention.

Family scenes.

Two-month-old cubs are called by Serena to share her kills. During the hunt itself, however, they are left hidden in cover.

Overleaf: Mara teaching her three cubs to hunt. The gazelle fawn had already been caught by her, but then released in front of the cubs so that they could practise catching and killing it. The cub with claws extended is attempting to deliver the tripping blow to knock the fawn off balance. While clearly inexperienced, it is a good illustration of how the cheetah uses its claws. Mara, second from the left, keeps an eye on the process.

While the loss of Sandy's family was a blow, we had the fortune to be in contact with another female and her cubs for an extended period. The mother in this was Mara, and she had given birth to five cubs a month or so before we arrived in the Game Reserve. We first saw them when they must have been about six weeks old – a week to ten days older than were Sandy's cubs when killed. They were already more mobile than Sandy's cubs had been and shortly after we first made their acquaintance Mara decided to move. The cubs were no longer parked in a lair to which she returned, but followed her wherever she went, except during the actual process of stalking and chasing. As soon as a kill was made Mara called them and they came up and shared it. The absence of a tie to a particular place enabled the family to drift eastward until by mid-January 1981 they were roaming the plains of Aitong, well outside the Game Reserve. These early days of mobility, when the cubs were between eight and ten weeks old, were fraught with danger. They were still a little wobbly and far from alert. Not being able to move fast they were vulnerable to many other predators. It did not surprise us when one cub disappeared soon after the family moved away from their natal area at the beginning of January 1981. On reaching the Aitong plains another cub was limping badly and within a week it, too, vanished. We think that the most likely cause will have been capture by a hyaena. Nevertheless, despite the hazards, the other three cubs grew apace. Each day saw them more alert and physically competent. By the end of January they had ceased to need milk and had been weaned.

The need to collect data from as many cheetahs as possible and the onset of the heavy rains in April caused us to divert our attention from Mara and her cubs for several months. We picked up with them again in June 1981 when they moved back into the Reserve close to where the cubs had been born on the Mara river (hence the mother's name). The youngsters were now about eight months old and all that remained of their juvenile pelage was a ruff about their necks. They were fully in control of themselves physically and honed their reflexes and toned their muscles through constant cat-like play with one another. As befits cheetahs there was rather more running and chasing than there was close-in wrestling. Mara sometimes joined her cubs romping, but most of the play was between the cubs themselves. Social grooming seemed, in the main, to be confined to licking one another's faces, particularly after feeding.

Until April 1981 the young were inactive during Mara's hunts. They would be parked while she stalked and chased and only rejoined her after the kill had been made. However, by the time that we rejoined this family in June of that year, the youngsters were showing a great interest in all their mother's hunting behaviour. This developed until they were attempting to take part. No longer would they remain quietly under a bush to watch; they had to go along. This produced a rather lean period for the family as, in most cases, the cubs' presence was more a hindrance than a help in hunting.

We watched a typical instance of bumbling on July 12th 1981. It was a sultry day and clouds built up all about us through the morning. Heavy rain started falling in the afternoon. This did not seem to inconvenience the cheetahs and, despite the deluge, Mara soon moved off from where they had been resting. The cubs romped about her as they went. After travelling along the rim of a luggah Mara stopped, head high, and stared across to the other side. Then, in a few quick strides she went across it and from her demeanour both we and the cubs knew she was going to hunt. When we caught up with her, Mara was watching a herd of impalas about one hundred paces distant and the cubs crouched in the luggah some ten steps behind her. The heavy rain helped to distract the quarry and Mara moved forward. Proceeding from bush to bush along the lip of the luggah she got within fifteen paces. The impalas were alert but oblivious of the cheetah poised nearby. Behind a small rise Mara readied herself for the rush: but she hadn't counted on her young. Down in the bottom of the luggah they couldn't see what was going on and became bored. They started to chase one another and one shot up the bank into full view of the impalas and they were off. Mara gave chase, but it was a disgusted, half-hearted effort that she soon abandoned.

Mara's greatly lowered kill rate, caused by the continual bumbling of the amateurs who dogged her, reached such a point in July that we feared for the family's health. In four consecutive days we witnessed no fewer than twelve unsuccessful hunts. The cubs' hunger and their inexperience led them to try for unusual quarry – with unexpected results. On one occasion they chased a buffalo and on another a zebra. In both cases the pursued turned and became the pursuers! The cheetahs had to flee. Mara also showed behaviour that has clearly evolved as an important teaching process. Twice we saw her catch a very young tommy fawn. In each instance she caught the victim by the head and not the usual throat grip. Holding it thus she waited until the cubs came up and then let it go. In both cases the fawns shot away with the cubs in hot pursuit, but although they kept up with them, they didn't seem to know what to do. Mara then outstripped them, tripped the fawns, grabbed them, held them, and then let them go again. The process was repeated over and over again until, eventually, the wretched victims were killed and eaten. Similar teaching behaviour has been reported from the Serengeti by George Frame. It seems an essential step in teaching the young cheetah how to fend for itself.

We watched another example of juvenile incompetence involving a female cheetah, Meta, and her almost fully grown cub. Lying on an anthill they watched a sounder of warthogs approaching: a sow and four small piglets. When they came within twenty paces of the cheetahs, the cub rushed them. Away went the hogs in line astern with their tails held high. The young cheetah managed to cut out the last one and head it away from the rest. Fast as warthogs are the cat was soon up with it when, to the cheetah's consternation, the piglet rounded and charged! Faced with an angry little hog that wasn't running away, the bold young predator braked to an abrupt halt and turned tail. Meta now came up and again the pig was off. A fast chase, out shot a forepaw, the piglet tumbled and was seized by the throat.

The arrival of the migrant wildebeest in late July ended the lean period in the Mara family's hunting fortunes. There were so many opportunities for killing that the learners' incompetence no longer had such a serious effect on the cheetahs' food supply. The wildebeest herds came with their annual crop of youngsters, all now six months old and weighing about thirty-six kilograms (80 pounds) – prime cheetah prey.

The technique the cheetahs used on the wildebeest herds was to make a concerted rush at a herd and then separate out a youngster during the resulting panicky flight. As soon as the wildebeest was isolated, Mara would make the final run and bring it down. The young cheetahs, now very much part of the team and growing in competence, often began to feed while Mara was still strangling the victim.

As Mara's cubs became more proficient hunters, they also became more adventurous. They continued to play and, having become accustomed to our vehicle, would jump all over it and stare through the windows into the interior, much to Nuggy's consternation. The scratches that they made in the paintwork with their blunt claws, were much appreciated reminders of the closeness we had developed with them. On one occasion their association produced an unwanted outcome. A pride of lions took an unexpected interest in our car, biting the front mudguard and trying to climb on top of the roof. Perhaps this was the outcome of having so much cheetah scent all over the vehicle?

As Mara's cubs grew older, our contacts with them grew fewer. It was unusual, however, when the family was joined by an adult male for a while. The cubs were eleven months old and it was possible that Mara might have been in oestrus, though she gave no sign of this that we could discern. The male left and the family stayed together for another four months. Then, on the 16th of February 1982, they were seen together for the last time. There had been little warning of the impending break and we saw no signs that we could appreciate. One day they were together, seemingly as close as they had been over the preceding year, the next they had gone their respective ways. Not only did the mother leave her young, but the young themselves parted company. We saw the male cub on his own on the 18th of February with no members of his family in sight and never saw the other four members of the family together again. They had gone their independent, feline ways.

Opposite: Another of Mara's cubs closing in and about to
make the trip in far more professional style.

Overleaf: Mara with three of her eleven month old cubs,
three months before the family broke up. At this stage it is
only the remnants of their neck ruffs that distinguish the
cubs from their mother to the casual glance.

Opposite: A young cheetah demonstrates the species' ability to climb while his litter mates play below.

Below and following pages: While the family is together, cheetah cubs play often, sparring, wrestling, mock fighting, and practising the trip.

119

A striking illustration of the manner in which cheetahs use their tails as counter-balances when making fast turns.

Opposite: Cheetahs can live without free water for long periods and do so regularly in the more arid parts of their ranges. However, in the Mara, where water is easily available, they drink often.

Overleaf: A golden haze symbolizes the Mara's misty future. For the moment all is well, but with growing pressures all about it, this state may not last.

Just as Mara's cubs grew up and went their separate ways, so too our interlude in the Reserve ran its course. Karl's dream that one had to live in the wilderness to appreciate it had been right. The difference between being a two-day tripper based in a tourist lodge and actually living in our own camp in the Reserve, was as great as riding a child's tricycle and flying in Concorde!

For all our appreciation of the Mara and getting to know it as we did, it is still difficult to define its attractions succinctly. The scenery is beautiful, but not unique. The wildlife spectacle is overwhelming at times, but so is it in parts of the southern Sudan and in the Antarctic. Perhaps the attractions have nothing to do with superlatives, but more with the simplicities of living in the bush. Our vision was unfettered by walls, nor bounded by windows; for most of the day we could see as far as the horizon and watch the sky's constantly changing perspectives and colours. The cruellest of an office's impositions must surely be the restriction of vision? Yet, if offices are to function, the natural world must be shut out, for the eye lighting on the flight of a bird, or on wind made visible through a field of grass, takes the mind off profits and losses. With freedom of vision goes freedom of mind, freedom to give attention to the attraction of the moment, to dwell in today with tomorrow taking care of itself. Perhaps one doesn't have to go to the Mara for all this; it could be this secret that gives country folk of the open air that calmness and placidity so rare among town people. No doubt we will speculate about our Mara idyll throughout our lives, drawing upon the memories now banked in our minds. Living out the experience was infinitely better than the dream that led to it.

We would like to think that, in our amateur way, we have repaid our Kenya benefactors in part for the great privilege of living in the Mara. We hope, too, that the information we gathered on cheetahs will add to the country's reservoir of knowledge, and that this book and its photographs will give to others some of the joy that we derived from our experiences. In particular, we desire that it will further interest in and understanding of cheetahs.

It would be nice to think that our observations will help the Mara to stay as we knew it in perpetuity. Yet this is unlikely. There are big changes afoot and we doubt that two generations hence it will be possible for anyone to repeat our experiences there. Many reasons support this view. In the first place it is becoming increasingly apparent that balance, in the sense of constancy, is not a feature of nature in Africa. More and more is it appreciated that change, constant change, is the name of the game. While man may play his part in the waxings and wanings of ecosystems, these trends have their roots in the great tides of nature, climatic cycles and the like. It is from this perspective that we realize that the Mara of our few short months is not the Mara of ten, twenty or fifty years ago. The huge population of wildebeest that now so dominates the landscape has risen in only two decades from just over three hundred thousand to one and a half million. A serious drought in the Serengeti-Mara region, a plague like rinderpest, could set back the animals' numbers to just a small fraction of what they currently are. When that happens, and most ecologists agree that such an event is likely sooner or later, then the plants and other animals will change as well. With a wildebeest crash will come a predator crash. The predator that we think will suffer the worst effects is likely to be the great cat that is least able to fend off its fellow predators. In this we take particular note of the fact that not one cheetah litter was reared successfully in the Mara's Talek area during our time in the Reserve. All perished due to other predators. For these reasons we wonder whether the 'right' places to conserve cheetahs as a species are in the dynamic, multifarious ecosystems such as the Serengeti-Mara, where dramatic changes are to be expected?

There are other grounds for our pessimism over the Mara Reserve. While there we saw evidence of poaching: five black rhinos were shot and two young ones died as a result of losing their mothers. Masai were implicated. We saw two impalas and a crocodile killed unlawfully. On the day that we arrived to set up camp, a gun battle between twenty-five Tanzanian rustlers and Kenyan forces took place in the Mara: twenty-two of the raiders were killed. Since then there have been several raids by bandits upon tourist facilities in and about the Reserve. Towards the end of the dry season in March 1982 the Masai, who lived across the Talek from our camp, had no grazing left in their pastures. For relief they brought their cattle into the Reserve. This was reported by visitors and conservationists, and the herdsmen were ordered out. However, it was a token gesture, for subsequently the cattle were brought into the Reserve during the hours of darkness, when prying visitors were confined to their camps and lodges.

The foregoing events can be viewed as incidents to be treated as they occurred; as events to be prevented from recurring through simple administrative measures. Yet seen in a wider perspective, each was the outcome of the dominant ecological force for change in modern Kenya: human population increase. Growing poverty seems an adjunct to more people. It provides a progressively greater incentive to poach and steal at the same time as there are more and more people becoming vulnerable to that incentive. Similarly there are more and more people to feed off the pastoral lands and an ever growing need for more land to be brought into production for humans. None of these trends bode well for the Mara.

The Masai, our nearest neighbours across the Talek, were under many pressures as a result of what is happening in Kenya. Through a young Masai man whom we employed to assist Daudi, we came to know these people well. Using our employee as interpreter, we learned their views and tried to impart some of ours. As a tribe the Masai have been the subject of much romantic attention by white people and described as examples of humans living in harmony with nature. For some centuries, at least, they and their forebears have lived off flocks that were herded among the wild plains species without overt conflict. Watching our friends' stock graze with zebras and gazelles in the daylight hours, listening to them returning each night in a pall of dust to the harmonious clinking of cattle bells, the bawling of calves, the calls of the herders, it would have been all too easy to delude ourselves that this Africa of the past might also be its future. Time and again we tried to capture these evening pastoral scenes on camera and sound track. And time and again we failed, for the aura of history and romance was beyond the capacity of film and sound tape to capture. Only the human mind seems able to record the nuances and all we can do now is to rely on our memories. It caused a deep ache to think that this beauty, this whole cattle culture, the lithe nonchalance and grace of its people, will not continue beyond the next few years.

Already the Masai are changing. Traditionally they have not eaten game meat. Yet when a cheetah killed an impala very close by our camp, some young men crossed the Talek and pirated all four legs off the kill for their own consumption. There are other signs. Less than twenty years ago permanent homesteads were unknown about the Mara. The pastoralists lived in temporary abodes fashioned from cowdung and withies. Being nomads, following rain, grasses and water, they had no need for permanent bases. But nomadism needs space and space is a vanishing commodity. Kenya's population, the fastest growing in the world, must be fed. This means more land under plough and hoe. Each acre taken over for cultivation means an acre less for the nomad or an acre less for wildlife. The division of Masailand into Group Ranches over the past ten years makes clear what is happening to the now open lands. The aim is to break down traditional Masai nomadism and have the people seek greater productivity through conventional ranching and farming. Formerly the entire Masai tribe owned their land jointly; now ownership is vested in groups and individuals with affiliations to particular areas. As nomadism collapses, in come the permanent dwellings, fences and the accoutrements of settled men – and out goes what is wild. The Mara becomes surrounded with homesteads and already thousands of acres of wheat ring the Mara's northern marches. Each year this cultivation spreads southwards, ever more confining upon stockmen who try to cling to the traditional way of life. To put a perspective of the future: it has been pointed out that by the year 2010 Kenya will have six million people surplus to those who can be accommodated on presently cultivated land. They will have to live somewhere. There are only two areas left in Kenya with reasonable agricultural potential – the Mara and a similarly sized area north of the Tana river delta. It is difficult to imagine that these areas will remain unoccupied. As it is, since we left the Mara, part of it has been de-gazetted as a Game Reserve and reverted to the local land users. What is perhaps of greatest importance, while there will be many who mourn the wild Mara's going, those who tame it will enter the land with gladness and the sense of right that characterises all frontiersmen.

The foregoing is of course an overview, of seeing the Mara in the context of wider events. While we were living there we did not have this perspective. Our Masai friends listened with kindly tolerance when we remonstrated with them over their cattle coming into the Reserve. We were unaware of the pressures for change that were upon them and the rapidly diminishing space that, previously, had been the essence of their romantic freedom. We suspect, too, that they also did not fully understand the changing course of events. No doubt they must have wondered why we, and other white people, made such a fuss about preserving game; why vast tracts had to be set aside for it and barred to the grazers who, for generations past, had lived among wildlife. These Masai must have been unimpressed by our arguments about tourism and the money it would bring (in all truth, our own experiences with tourism qualify it as a necessary evil at best, and *not* a highly desirable development!). Further, they patiently pointed out to us that the Mara Reserve was there because they, themselves, had agreed that it should be established. Now, alas, it was the millstone against which they were being crushed by the development and expansion elsewhere! It is indeed ironic that they have to poach grazing in the dead of night which, had they refused to agree to the creation of the Reserve, was theirs anyway.

We believe that there will come a time when the Mara Reserve will change to the point when it will be of no consequence in the preservation of cheetahs as a species. However, we do not think that this will presage their extinction generally. The cheetahs' strongholds will always be in the great arid gazelle lands of northern Kenya and the Horn of Africa, in large tracts of Sahelia and in the Kalahari and its environs. Even with the most advanced technology, man will never easily settle these lands and to use them will still have to be a nomad. In such vast dry regions, so open and suited to the species' particular mode of hunting, its adaptations and its ability to do without water, cheetahs will probably hold their own against the other species that so dominate it in lusher lands. The latest information from a Kenya-wide survey shows that cheetahs are maintaining their numbers successfully in the arid zones and that earlier predictions of them being on the verge of extinction are, happily, untrue.

Like animals of the desert or semi-desert, cheetahs inhabiting the dry lands will never be readily observed. They will be spaced apart and their densities determined by the low numbers and widespread distributions of their prey. But will that be a bad thing? Does an animal have to be on show or is it enough that it simply exists?

It has been said recently that cheetah males, generally, suffer from low fertility and that this may be a factor complicating their conservation. Future research may confirm this, but we believe that it is highly unlikely that it can be a sudden development throughout their range over hundreds of thousands of square kilometres. What is more likely is that an inherent feature of cheetah reproductive physiology has been discovered and that while sperm counts may seem low in comparison with other cats, they may be the norm for cheetahs.

We will mourn the end of the Mara when it happens, for with it will go part of our hearts. The loss of the region's cheetahs will be particularly poignant for they contributed so much to our lives. However, just as the loss of Sandy's cubs hurt deeply at the time but didn't mean the end of the population, so the fortunes of the Mara will not spell the end of the cheetahs. These, the most elegant of the world's cats, are well equipped to survive elsewhere. Their chances are infinitely better than those of the forest species whose habitats man can occupy and change forever.

Right: Modern tourism adopts many forms. Game viewing from balloons is one of the more bizarre. Others, however, may not have so mild an impact on environments. Tourists, themselves, become a threat to the wild when their numbers exceed certain levels.

Overleaf: Impala have no place in the wheat fields which encroach the Mara's borders.

An idyllic pastoral scene on the Talek shows Masai as they were. In this state they did not compete much with plains wildlife. With their entry into the mainstreams of modern life and the world's cash economy, and their rapid growth in numbers, unavoidably they will become less tolerant of it.

Overleaf: A sphinx at sunset: yet another vignette of the Mara we like to remember.

## Background Facts

### The Cheetah's Taxonomic Status

Order: Carnivora          Family: Felidae
Genus: Acinonyx          Species: Jubatus
Scientific name: *Acinonyx jubatus*

### Evolution

The palaeontological record suggests that the genus *Acinonyx* first emerged as a distinctive felid form in the Pliocene. Three species are known to have existed: *A. pardinensis*, a large form distributed across Europe, India and China in the Lower Pleistocene; *A. intermedius*, a smaller form, more Asian than European, in the Middle Pleistocene; and *A. jubatus*, the extant species in the Upper Pleistocene and Holocene, of Asia and Africa.

### Present Distribution

A small population in Iran and widely across sub-Saharan Africa in open country that is not settled by cultivators or under arable agriculture.

### Conservation Status

From the early years of this century cheetahs were thought to be in numerical decline over most of their range. This belief became widely accepted. Estimates of total numbers ranged from 8,000 to 25,000. However, other than in a few national parks, these estimates were guesswork and unsubstantiated. Recent studies suggest that the species' status is not as critical as was thought and that loss of range over past 20 years in East Africa has been slight. In places where sheep and goats are not closely herded, e.g. in Namibia and Eastern Kenya, cheetah are considered a nuisance. Where studied in East African wildlife sanctuaries, cheetahs seem particularly vulnerable to other large predators. Trade in cheetahs and their skins is internationally prohibited under the Convention on International Trade in Endangered Species of Fauna and Flora (CITES).

## Recommended Cheetah Reading

Burney, D. A. 1980. The effects of Human Activities on Cheetahs (*Acinonyx jubatus* Schr.) in the Mara Region of Kenya. M.Sc. Thesis, University of Nairobi.

Eaton, R. L. 1974. *The Cheetah, the Biology, Ecology and Behaviour of an Endangered Species.* Van Nostrand Reinhold Company, New York.

Frame, G., and Frame, L. 1981. *Swift and Enduring: Cheetahs and Wild Dogs of the Serengeti.* Elsevier & Dutton Publications Inc., New York.

Graham, A. D. 1966. East African Wildlife Society Cheetah Survey, *East African Wildlife Journal*, Vol. 4.

Kingdon, J. 1977. *East African Mammals*, Vol. IIIA. Academic Press, London.

Schaller, G. B. 1973. *Serengeti – A Kingdom of Predators.* Collins, London.

Wrogeman, N. 1975. *Cheetah Under the Sun.* McGraw-Hill Book Company, Johannesburg.